Why's Snot Sticky?

This edition published in 2022 by Arcturus Publishing Limited
26/27 Bickels Yard, 151–153 Bermondsey Street,
London SE1 3HA

Illustrator: Luke Séguin-Magee
Authors: William Potter and Helen Otway
Editors: Susie Rae and Joe Harris
Designer: Rosie Bellwood

CH008348NT
Supplier: 10, Date 0522, Print run 000001551

Printed in the UK

MIX
Paper from
responsible sources
FSC® C018072
FSC
www.fsc.org

CONTENTS

ARE YOU FEELING WELL? YOU SOON WON'T BE!

THIS FREAKY FACT BOOK IS FULL OF DEADLY DISEASES, BEASTLY BACTERIA, WRIGGLY WORMS, AND THINGS THAT MAKE YOU ITCH.

If you've ever wanted to know more about how your body works, how it can go terribly wrong, and why it smells like it does, you're in the right place. Now, please stop picking that—it'll go septic!

SPIT, SNOT, AND TEARS

HOW FAST IS A SNEEZE?

When you sneeze, the air coming out of your nose and mouth travels at the same speed as a category-2 hurricane: 160km (100 miles) an hour!

WHAT'S BETTER, SMELL OR TASTE?

Your sense of smell is 10,000 times more sensitive than your sense of taste. About 80 percent of what you taste comes from what you can smell, which is why you don't taste much at all if you have a cold!

WHY ARE FARTS NOISY?

What you hear when you fart is the vibration of your sphincter muscles as air passes through them. The sort of sound you get depends on how fast the air is going.

DID YOU KNOW?

You have more bacteria on your body than there are people in the world.

WHAT'S THE POINT OF YAWNING?

Yawning is your body's way of getting more oxygen into your lungs to try to make you feel more awake.

HOW DO ASTRONAUTS BRUSH THEIR TEETH?

In space, astronauts use specially formulated non-toxic toothpaste, because they have to swallow all the froth. Gross!

DO YOU SWEAT ALL THE TIME?

You sweat all day long, even when you don't feel it. As you read this, more than two million sweat glands around your body are working to keep it at the right temperature.

DID YOU KNOW?

Your fingerprints, palm prints, tongue print, toe prints, and sole prints are all unique!

HOW MUCH SKIN DO YOU GROW?

Your body makes a new skin every month—that means you'll get through about 1,000 skins in your lifetime!

ARE POISONS GOOD FOR THE SKIN?

Poisons can give you great-looking skin! Botulinum toxin (Botox) is famous for its wrinkle-smoothing effects, but for those who don't like needles, there is a cream that mimics viper venom and gives similar results.

WHY DO THINGS LOOK BLURRY UNDERWATER?

The lenses in your eyes are designed to focus the light in air. Water bends light so that your eyes can't focus it properly—that's why everything's blurred if you keep your eyes open underwater!

HOW MUCH SPIT DO YOU MAKE IN A DAY?

You produce a lot of saliva—about 1 L (2pt) a day. A cow produces 150 times more!

IS BIRD POOP GOOD FOR YOU?

Fancy a Japanese bird poop facial? The special enzymes in the droppings of the Japanese bush warbler make it an ingredient in some anti-wrinkle treatments.

WHEN IS THE BEST TIME OF DAY TO SNIFF?

Your sense of smell is better during the day than first thing in the morning.

DID YOU KNOW?

Humans live longer than any other mammals on the planet.

WHAT IS THE MOST COMMON EYE SHADE?

Most of the world's population has brown eyes. In the US, only one person in six has blue eyes, compared to every other person a century ago. Where did all those blue eyes go?!

DO SOME PEOPLE HAVE TONGUES LIKE SNAKES?

The most bizarre cosmetic procedure has to be tongue-splitting. A cut is made down the middle of the tongue to give it a forked appearance. Freaky!

DID YOU KNOW?

Your fingerprints were formed six months before you were born.

WHAT DOES COLA DO TO YOUR TEETH?

Cola is more acidic than vinegar—and acid destroys the enamel on your teeth, so remember to brush properly!

WHY IS SNOT STICKY?

Another word for snot is mucus. Mucus is made by cells in many part of your body, including your nose, lungs, and digestive system. It's sticky because its job is to trap things that shouldn't be in your body—such as harmful bacteria, pollen, dust, and fungi.

HOW BUSY ARE YOUR EYE MUSCLES?

Your eye muscles just can't keep still—they move more than 100,000 times a day, and are even busy while you're asleep!

DID YOU KNOW?

Your sense of hearing is at its best when you are 10 years old.

DID YOU KNOW?

Some perfumes contain something called ambergris. Think it sounds nice? It's whale vomit!

WHY IS SWEAT SMELLY?

Sweat is made mainly of water, so it doesn't smell ... until it's been around for a while. Once skin bacteria have had time to slurp it up and multiply, the whiff begins.

ARE ALL TEARS THE SAME?

Your eyes produce three sorts of tears—basal tears to keep the eyes moist, reflex tears when you get something in your eyes, and psychic tears when you cry with sadness, happiness, or pain.

CAN YOU GROW SKIN IN A LAB?

A new sheet of skin can be grown from just a few of your cells. New skin is grown in special laboratories, and is used to replace damaged skin in a skin graft operation.

DID YOU KNOW?

If you cut yourself, your body will produce more than a million extra cells each hour until the wound heals.

HOW MUCH TIME DO WE SPEND KISSING?

Over your lifetime, you will spend a whole two weeks kissing. Though hopefully not all at once!

WHY DO YOUR LIPS GET DRY?

Sebum is the oily stuff secreted by glands in your skin to keep it soft. The only part of your body that doesn't have any is your lips—that's why they dry out easily.

WHAT IS A BELLY BUTTON?

Your belly button is the scar left from your umbilical cord. Whether it's an "innie" or an "outie" depends on the shape and size of your umbilical cord when you were born.

HOW LONG DO TASTE BUDS LAST?

Each of your taste buds lasts for just over a week! They are most quickly replaced when you are young.

IS IT NORMAL TO HAVE SWEATY FEET?

Yes. In fact, the 250,000 sweat glands in your feet make them one of the sweatiest parts of your body. Adults produce two whole cups of that stinky foot juice every week!

WHO HAS THE MOST HAIR— BLONDES OR BRUNETTES?

Fair-haired people have more hairs on their head than dark-haired people.

IS ALL FAT THE SAME?

You have two types of fat under your skin and around your organs—white adipose tissue and brown adipose tissue. They both keep you warm, but the brown fat gives extra insulation, so you had more of it when you were born than you do now.

DID YOU KNOW?

A bloodhound's sense of smell is thousands of times more sensitive than that of a human.

DID YOU KNOW?

You have more pain sensors in your skin than any other type of sensor.

DID YOU KNOW?

You have a whole nervous system just to control your bowels.

WHAT HAPPENS TO MOST OF YOUR SNOT?

Your nose is busy making mucus all day long, but you swallow most of it—about one cupful a day. Gross!

WHAT'S MORE DANGEROUS—SHARKS OR COCONUTS?

Falling coconuts kill 10 times more people than sharks do every year.

DID YOU KNOW?

Your nails grow more quickly as you get older.

DOES EVERYONE HAVE A DIFFERENT VOICE?

No one in the world has the same voiceprint as you. Your larynx, nose, and mouth shape all affect the way you speak, so your voice is completely unique.

WHO HAS THE MOST NOSE HAIR?

Men have more nose hair than women ... and it grows longer as they get older!

WHY DO YOU FEEL A BUMP BEFORE YOU FEEL PAIN?

Touch signals travel to the brain more quickly than pain signals. That's why you feel the bump from stubbing your toe before the agony sets in!

WHY DO DENTISTS HAVE TO SCRAPE YOUR TEETH?

It takes six hours for a coating of plaque to form after cleaning your teeth. If you don't brush it off, it eventually becomes tartar— a rock-hard substance that your dentist has to scrape off.

HOW MUCH DO YOU FLAKE?

In the last minute, at least 40,000 dead skin cells came off your body. You lose about 50 million of them every day. If your dead skin cells didn't drop off, after three years your skin would be as thick as an elephant's!

WHAT IS DROOL MADE OF?

Your saliva is made up of 99 percent water.

WHY DOES YOUR NOSE RUN WHEN YOU CRY?

Your tear ducts go from your eyes to your nose. That's why your nose runs when you cry, and why you can sometimes taste eye drops.

HOW MUCH HAIR DO YOU LOSE EACH DAY?

Each hair on your head grows for up to six years. Then it stops, hangs around for a while, and eventually drops out. About 50-100 hairs drop out of your head every day, but that still leaves you with more than 99,900 to brush while new ones grow!

DID YOU KNOW?

When you were born, you could only see about 30cm (12in) past the end of your nose.

CAN YOU CRY IN SPACE?

It's impossible to cry in space—the lack of gravity means that tears can't trickle!

DO ONLY TONGUES HAVE TASTE BUDS?

Taste buds aren't just on your tongue—there are more than 2,000 of your them in your throat and on the roof of your mouth.

DID YOU KNOW?

Nobody's eyes are quite like yours! Your iris has 256 unique characteristics—more than your fingerprint, which only has 40.

DID YOU KNOW?

Right-handed people tend to chew food on the right side of their mouth, while left-handed people chew more on the left.

WHY DOES BLUSHING MAKE YOU FEEL HOT?

You feel hot when you blush because you're blushing all over! Embarrassment triggers a rush of blood through all your blood vessels, even the ones in your stomach.

WHEN ARE MOST BABIES BORN?

More of the world's babies are born in August than in any other month.

DO BABIES CRY TEARS?

Newborn babies don't cry tears. It takes a few weeks for their tear glands to start working.

DID YOU KNOW?

If you ate nothing but carrots, your skin would turn orange!

DO ANY ANIMALS HAVE FINGERPRINTS LIKE OURS?

A koala's fingerprints look very similar to a human's. If a crime scene smells of eucalyptus, it was definitely the koala that did it!

DID YOU KNOW?

A dead body has to be put in a fridge so it doesn't go off! Bodies in a morgue are kept at a temperature of 2-4°C (35-39°F).

DID YOU KNOW?

You have mucus in your eyes! It's there to make your tear fluid spread evenly.

CAN YOU FREEZE YOUR BODY AFTER DEATH?

People can choose to have their bodies deep frozen after death in case scientists come up with a way of bringing them back to life ... but they will have to pay around £150,000/ US$200,000 for the privilege.

DO EARS KEEP ON GROWING?

Although your ears will grow throughout your life, your hearing will just get worse. What a bad design!

WHERE IS YOUR SKIN THE THINNEST?

Your skin is at its thinnest on your eyelids, and at its thickest on the soles of your feet.

HOW MANY EYELASHES DO WE GROW IN OUR LIFETIME?

If you kept all your loose eyelashes and lined them up, they would stretch for around 30m (100ft). Hopefully you'll find better ways to spend your retirement!

DID YOU KNOW?

The little pink lump in the corner of your eye is what remains of an extra eyelid that our ancient ancestors once had.

WHERE IN YOUR BODY IS THERE NO BLOOD?

Your eye's cornea is the only part of your body that has no blood supply, since it needs to be clear for you to see through it. What it does have is lots of nerve endings—that's why a scratch in your eye is so painful.

IS HAIR ALIVE?

The hairs that you can see are dead, which is why it doesn't hurt when you have a haircut. They have sensors on the roots, though, so it hurts if someone pulls them!

DID YOU KNOW?

If you're right-handed, you will sweat most under your right arm. If you're left-handed, you're more likely to get a wet patch under your left arm!

Your salivary glands (which produce spit) slow down when you're asleep, which is why you wake up with a dry mouth and stinky breath!

WHAT GROWS FASTER—FINGERNAILS OR TOENAILS?

Fingernails grow four times faster than toenails. Your fastest growing nail is the one on your middle finger.

HOW DOES SOAP WORK?

Soap works by sticking to dirt particles so that they come away from the skin. You can see the difference by washing dirty hands with just water first!

DID YOU KNOW?

Being too hot or too cold in bed increases your chances of having bad dreams.

CAN YOUR HAIR TURN WHITE FROM SHOCK?

It's impossible for hair to turn white from shock. What can happen, though, is that a shock makes pigmented hair suddenly fall out, so someone with a mixture of brown and white hair would then be left with only white hairs.

WHO BLINKS THE MOST?

Over your lifetime, you will blink 650 million times. Women blink more than men, and adults blink more than children. Newborn babies blink only once or twice a minute!

DID YOU KNOW?

One in three people will have a surgical operation in their lifetime.

DID YOU KNOW?

Sticky earwax glows in ultraviolet light.

HOW FAST DO BEARDS GROW?

Men need to shave so often because beard hair grows faster than any other body hair. If a man let his beard grow forever, it could reach a length of more than 9m (28ft).

HOW MANY SMELLS CAN YOU SENSE?

Your nose is so sensitive that it can identify more than 10,000 different smells.

DID YOU KNOW?

Your teeth are protected by enamel, which is the hardest substance in your body.

DO TWINS HAVE THE SAME FINGERPRINTS?

Although identical twins have the same DNA, their fingerprints are different.

HOW LONG HAVE HUMANS HAD TATTOOS?

Tattoos have been around for thousands of years—there were 57 on the body of a mummified man discovered in the Austrian Alps, dating from 3300 BCE.

DID YOU KNOW?

You cannot sneeze with your eyes open.

WHAT ARE FINGERNAILS MADE OF?

They may look different, but your hair and fingernails are made from the same stuff—keratin. It's what a cow's horns and a lion's claws are made from, too!

ARE GORILLAS HAIRIER THAN HUMANS?

Humans and gorillas are both covered with around five million hairs; the difference is that ape hair is much thicker and longer.

INSIDE OUT

CAN YOU DRINK YOUR OWN PEE?

There are no harmful bacteria in fresh urine, so it's perfectly safe to drink. Safe? Yes. Disgusting? Absolutely!

HOW STRESSFUL IS BEING BORN?

Being born is really stressful! As you came into the world, you had higher levels of the stress hormone adrenaline in your body than an adult would have during a heart attack.

WHERE HAS YOUR BLOOD GONE?

Only four percent of your blood is in your heart right now. The rest is racing around your body!

DID YOU KNOW?

Your body is made up of more than 230 joints.

DO WE HAVE METAL BODIES?

You have several different metals in your body, such as iron in your blood and potassium in your nervous system. Calcium is what you have the most of—that's what makes your bones and teeth hard.

WHY IS POOP BROWN?

What gives poop its normal shade is bilirubin, a brown substance that comes from the breakdown of old blood cells in the liver.

WHY ARE BRAINS SO DEMANDING?

Your brain is a very demanding organ—it uses one-fifth of your body's blood, oxygen, and energy supplies.

DO ATHLETES HAVE BIGGER HEARTS?

People who exercise too much can develop "athletic heart syndrome," where the heart becomes enlarged from having to pump extra blood around the body.

ARE SOME OF YOUR MUSCLES OUT OF CONTROL?

You can control some of your muscles, but others are doing their own thing! Your involuntary muscles control bodily functions, such as heartbeat and digestion.

HOW MUCH DUST DO YOU SWALLOW?

You will breathe in around 18kg (40lb) of dust over your lifetime—that's about 18 large bags of flour!

DO WE HAVE TAILS?

You have a tailbone at the end of your spine! It is called the coccyx—meaning "cuckoo"—because it looks like a cuckoo's beak.

DID YOU KNOW?

If a person's liver stops working, they will die within 24 hours.

HOW CAN YOU TRAIN TO BE A SWORD-SWALLOWER?

Sword-swallowers train themselves to control the gag reflex that occurs when something touches the soft palate at the back of the mouth. If you touch it, you'll vomit ... so don't try it!

HOW OFTEN DOES YOUR HEART BEAT?

Your heart is busy every second of the day. It beats around 35 million times a year.

HOW LONG ARE YOUR INTESTINES?

If you took out your intestines and uncoiled them, they would be about four times as tall as you.

DO YOU LOSE BONES AS YOU GROW UP?

Yes! When you were born you had more than 300 bones, but you'll have only 206 by the time you finish growing! Don't worry, you won't completely lose them along the way—some of your smaller bones just fuse together to make bigger bones.

DID YOU KNOW?

When you feel thirsty, your body is already dehydrated. It's your brain's way of telling you to get a drink, quick!

DID YOU KNOW?

Your tiniest blood vessels are called capillaries. You have more than 10 billion and they're so narrow that red blood cells have to travel down them in single file!

WHERE ARE YOUR LARGEST MUSCLES?

You sit on the largest muscles in your body! You have a gluteus maximus in each buttock.

WHY SHOULD YOU NOT SAY "BONE DRY"?

Your bones are not as dry as you might think—they are made up of 20 percent water. Your biggest bones are soft inside! They contain jelly-like bone marrow, which makes three million new blood cells every second.

DO DEAD BODIES FART?

When a dead body is decomposing, the bacteria inside it produce gases. When the gas is released from the body, it sounds like a fart!

WHAT IS PLASMA?

More than half of your blood is made up of plasma, a pale yellow fluid containing nutrients, proteins, and waste products.

WHY IS PUKE GREEN?

When you have a bad tummy bug, you will eventually throw up green vomit. The shade comes from bile, which is deep down in the stomach and comes up only when nothing else is left.

CAN YOUR BRAIN FEEL PAIN?

The brain cannot feel pain, so some brain surgery can be done while the patient is awake! The surgeon will then talk to the patient during the operation to make sure that healthy parts of the brain are not being affected.

ARE BOTH OF YOUR LUNGS IDENTICAL?

Your lungs are not the same. The right one has three lobes (sections), while the left one has only two and is slightly smaller, to make room for your heart.

DO BRAINS FLOAT?

Your brain is surrounded by a liquid called cerebrospinal fluid. It cushions the brain to protect it from bumps and sudden movements. It constantly needs topping up, so fluid is being made by your body all the time.

DID YOU KNOW?

Make your hand into a fist— that's how big your heart is!

DID YOU KNOW?

You have three sorts of rib—true ribs are attached to your spine and breastbone, false ribs are attached to your spine and lowest true ribs, and floating ribs are attached to only the spine. No spare ribs, though!

ARE THERE BUGS IN YOUR BODY?

Yes—if you mean bacteria! There are actually more than 700 kinds of bacteria lurking in your intestine.

WHAT DO BRAINS FEEL LIKE?

If you could touch your brain, it would feel like jelly!

DID YOU KNOW?

By the time each of your red blood cells dies, it has been around your body 250,000 times.

CAN YOU HAVE EXTRA KIDNEYS?

You probably have two kidneys ... but you could have more. People with extra kidneys don't find out until they have a scan for other problems. British teenager Laura Moon discovered she had four kidneys when she had a scan for stomach pains!

WHAT IS THE LONGEST BONE IN YOUR BODY?

The longest bone in your body is your femur, or thighbone. The thighbone of the tallest man ever was around 72cm (2ft 5in) long!

CAN HUMANS USE PIG HEARTS?

Pig hearts are similar to ours, so pig heart valves are sometimes used in open-heart surgery to replace faulty human ones.

DID YOU KNOW?

A really big sneeze can make you fracture a rib.

WHY DOES ASPARAGUS MAKE YOUR PEE SMELL?

If you eat asparagus, your urine might smell of rotten cabbages! The whiff comes from a gas called methanethiol, which is produced when you digest the vegetable.

IS THERE A POOP CHART?

If you ever want to classify what you leave behind in the toilet, you should take a look at the Bristol Stool Chart. The seven types of stool listed range from "separate hard lumps, like nuts" (Type 1) to "entirely liquid" (Type 7).

DID YOU KNOW?

Your body cannot digest tomato seeds—they pass straight through your intestines. Eat some today and see for yourself!

WHERE ARE MOST OF YOUR BONES?

Almost half of the bones in your body are in your hands and feet.

WHERE IS YOUR BODY'S SMALLEST MUSCLE?

The smallest muscle in your body is deep inside your ear. It's joined to the smallest bone in your body— the stirrup.

DID YOU KNOW?

There is so much electrical activity going on in your brain that you could power a light bulb with it!

WHY DO TUMMIES RUMBLE?

Does your tummy ever rumble or growl? The proper name for it is borborygmus and it's the sound of muscles contracting in your digestive system.

CAN MUSCLES PUSH?

Muscles can only pull, not push. To move your arm in two directions, you have muscles to pull it one way ... then different muscles to pull it the other way!

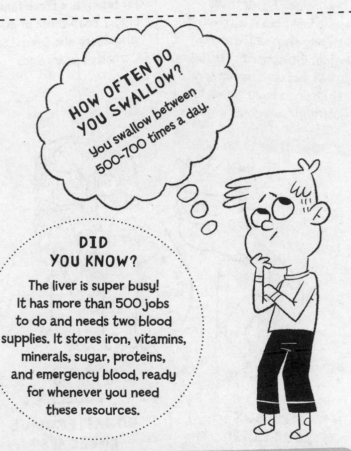

HOW OFTEN DO YOU SWALLOW?

You swallow between 500-700 times a day.

DID YOU KNOW?

The liver is super busy! It has more than 500 jobs to do and needs two blood supplies. It stores iron, vitamins, minerals, sugar, proteins, and emergency blood, ready for whenever you need these resources.

HOW MUCH DO YOU PEE IN A LIFETIME?

All those quick trips to the bathroom add up to about 45,000 L (95,000pt) of urine over a lifetime. That would fill a swimming pool!

WHAT DOES THE INSIDE OF AN INTESTINE LOOK LIKE?

The inside of your small intestine looks like it is covered with tiny fingers! These villi give your intestine the largest possible surface area for you to get the maximum amount of nutrition from your food.

ARE HUMAN BRAINS BIGGER THAN THEIR ANCESTORS'?

Our brains are three times bigger than those of our ancestors who lived 2.5 million years ago.

WHAT IS MOST OF YOUR BRAIN MADE OF?

Your brain is about 75 percent water. That's why you should always make sure you drink enough.

DO BABIES HAVE KNEECAPS?

Newborn babies have no kneecaps. The triangular patella bones don't develop until after two years of age.

DO SURGEONS LEAVE THINGS INSIDE BODIES?

Foreign bodies can occasionally get left behind during operations. Things that have been sewn inside patients include clamps, surgical sponges, scalpels, scissors, and forceps.

DID YOU KNOW?

You have more red blood cells than any other type of cell.

WHAT ARE "BUTTERFLIES?"

The "butterflies" you feel when you're excited or scared are muscles tightening inside your tummy.

WHAT IS VOMIT?

Vomit is a yucky cocktail of half-digested food, stomach mucus, saliva, and gastric acids.

HOW LONG DOES FOOD STAY IN YOUR BODY?

Most of the food you eat spends between one and three hours in your stomach, but fatty foods hang around for longer.

DID YOU KNOW?

Two million tiny nephrons in your kidneys are filtering your blood as you read this!

DID YOU KNOW?

About 0.01 percent of the population has internal organs on the opposite side to everyone else, with no ill effects.

WHAT IS HEARTBURN?

Heartburn has nothing to do with the heart. It's the burning pain of stomach acid leaking back into your gullet, or food pipe.

DO YOU JUMP IN YOUR SLEEP?

If you ever jump suddenly when you're falling asleep, you're experiencing a hypnic jerk. As your body relaxes, the brain mistakes the nerve messages for a falling sensation, and stiffens the body to get it upright again.

DID YOU KNOW?

About 1L (2pt) of blood passed through your liver in the last minute!

HOW ACIDIC IS YOUR STOMACH?

The pH level in your stomach is 1 or 2, which is more acidic than vinegar. Although your gastric juices contain powerful acids, they cannot digest chewing gum. Small amounts will get through the digestive system, but too much can cause a serious blockage ... so always spit it out.

DID YOU KNOW?

Your heart first started beating eight months before you were born.

HOW MANY MUSCLES DO YOU HAVE?

You have more than 630 muscles in your body. Even if you're sitting still, lots of muscles are working to do things like make you breathe and keep your blood flowing. Reading this uses your eye muscles, too!

HOW FAST IS A COUGH?

When you cough, air rushes through your windpipe at 100km/h (60 mph).

DID YOU KNOW?

Only a few hundred people in the world have the rarest blood type, which is H-H. They can't receive blood transfusions from any other blood group, so sometimes need to store their own blood before an operation.

HOW FAR DOES YOUR BLOOD TRAVEL?

Your blood goes on a 19,000-km (12,000-mile) journey every day!

HOW FAST ARE NERVE SIGNALS?

Nerve signals travel incredibly fast—a nerve message from your toe will reach your brain in less than one hundredth of a second.

DID YOU KNOW?

You have slimy mucus in your stomach. It stops the acidic digestive juices burning the stomach lining and protects it from enzymes. If you didn't have this mucus, you'd digest yourself!

DID YOU KNOW?

A pinhead-sized piece of your brain contains 60,000 nerve cells called neurons.

WHY SHOULD YOU EAT SOMETHING YOU CAN'T DIGEST?

You can't digest fiber (also spelled fibre), which is in fruit, vegetables, and whole foods. So why bother eating it? Because it keeps your digestive system running smoothly.

DID YOU KNOW?

After being removed from the body, the lungs can survive longer than any other organ.

HOW MANY CELLS ARE IN A DROP OF BLOOD?

There are over 5 million blood cells in a tiny drop of blood.

DID YOU KNOW?

Did you know that your bones are alive? They're full of living cells, which is why they can mend themselves. If you could look inside your bones, you would see that they're full of holes— just like a sponge! If your bones were solid, they would be too heavy to move about.

WHAT'S A "BRAIN FREEZE?"

A "brain freeze" headache occurs when cold food or drink in your mouth triggers a nerve message to the brain that says you're in a cold environment. Your blood vessels suddenly swell to warm you up ... and it hurts!

WHY SHOULD YOU USE SUNBLOCK?

Sunburn damages your blood vessels so badly that it takes them months to repair themselves. It can also cause permanent damage, including skin cancer, so you should always protect your skin from the sun.

HOW CAN LAUGHING HELP YOU BEAT A TEST?

Laughing cancels out the hormones in your body that make you feel stressed, so if you have a test coming up, just laugh about it!

WHY ARE TOILETS NO USE?

Most modern toilets are not well designed for their purpose, as the best body position for passing a stool is squatting, not sitting.

WHAT ARE NEURONS?

Neurons carry nerve messages to and from your brain. The tiniest ones are smaller than a pencil dot, while the longest ones are 1m (3ft) long!

HOW DO YOU VOMIT?

When you vomit, the muscles in your stomach and intestines go into reverse: instead of pushing the food down, they push it up and out of your mouth.

BODY INVADERS

WHAT DO HEAD LICE FEED ON?

Head lice slurp blood from your scalp! Don't panic, they're so tiny that you won't feel a thing. Girls are more likely to have head lice than boys, as they tend to have longer hair.

HOW SHARP ARE FUNNEL-WEB SPIDER FANGS?

The aggressive Australasian funnel web spider has such sharp fangs that they can pierce through fingernails and soft shoes.

WHY ARE HEAD LICE HARD TO SPOT?

Don't think that you can spot head lice more easily in light hair—those critters can change shade to merge with their surroundings.

54

ARE THERE BLOODSUCKERS IN YOUR BED?

Bedbugs are the vampires of the pest world—they hate sunlight and prefer to venture out to bite you at night.

ARE THERE EGGS IN YOUR CLOTHES?

African tumbu flies lay their eggs in clothing. The eggs hatch on contact with human skin and the larvae burrow under the skin's surface, creating boil-like sores to grow in.

DID YOU KNOW?

A spitting cobra will defend itself by shooting poison into an attacker's eyes, causing agonizing pain and leaving them temporarily blind.

DO BATS LIKE UNDERWEAR?

When hotel receptionist Abbie Hawkins felt something moving on her chest while she was at work, she had a look and found a baby bat nestled inside her bra! The bat-hiding underwear had been left on the washing line the previous night.

IS RINGWORM ACTUALLY A WORM?

No! Ringworm is actually a type of fungal infection which causes a circular rash on your skin.

HOW LONG CAN TAPEWORMS GROW?

A broad tapeworm can grow in the intestine for decades, reaching a length of 10m (33ft). Worst of all, you may not even know you have one!

WHAT SMELL DO MOSQUITOES HATE?

Mosquitoes hate the smell of garlic, so you can try eating some to keep them at bay. Plus, you can ward off vampires at the same time!

WHAT CARRIES THE MOST DISEASE?

The common housefly carries more diseases than any other creature in the world.

DID YOU KNOW?

Some tapeworm eggs can grow into a cyst as large as a grapefruit! It's not common, though, so don't have nightmares.

CAN YOU GET BUGS IN YOUR EYEBROWS?

Demodex mites are tiny parasites that live in eyebrows and eyelashes. They're very common, especially in older people. Under a microscope, they look like worms with stubby legs.

DOES EVERYONE CARRY PARASITES?

Parasites are happily living in at least 75 percent of the world's population.

DID YOU KNOW?

While mosquitoes puncture the skin and suck up blood, horseflies get to your blood by taking a chunk out of your skin with their serrated jaws.

WHY SHOULD YOU BEWARE OF RAT PEE?

Weil's disease is a serious infection carried in rats' urine. It is usually caught from infected water.

WHAT IS CREEPING ERUPTION?

Gnathostoma spinigerum is a worm that wriggles around under the skin, causing an itchy, snake-shaped rash known as creeping eruption.

WHAT BUG LIKES SIPPING TEARS?

Eye gnats love to slurp up tear fluid, so will lurk around your eye area while waiting for a drink.

CAN YOU CATCH WORMS FROM PETS?

Many dogs and cats have worms that you can catch through contact with their poop.

CAN HUMAN POOP BE USED FOR FERTILIZER?

Human sewage is sometimes used to fertilize fields in developing countries, but it can be full of worm eggs. When the egg-infested vegetables are eaten, worm infections are spread even further.

WHY SHOULD YOU NOT SCRATCH THREADWORM EGGS?

The female threadworm lays between 10,000 and 20,000 eggs at a time on its human host's bottom. She then spreads around a secretion that causes itching, to make the host scratch at the eggs and share them with friends.

WHAT CAUSES A ZIG-ZAG PATTERN ON YOUR SKIN?

The tiny scabies mite tunnels beneath the skin in a zig-zag shape, causing unbearable itching.

DID YOU KNOW?

Only female midges and mosquitoes bite people. If a wasp stings you, it's female too.

COULD VAMPIRES BATS SUCK YOUR BLOOD?

Believe it or not, they could! Until recently scientists thought that hairy-legged vampire bats only drank birds' blood, but in 2017 they discovered that humans are on the menu, too.

COULD A FURRY CATERPILLAR MAKE SOMEONE BLEED TO DEATH?

Yes. The venom released by the hairs on a South American silk moth caterpillar stops blood from clotting. As a result, an unlucky human victim could bleed to death if bitten.

ARE WORMS SCARY?

Helmintophobia is a fear of getting worms. Hands up anyone who isn't scared!

HOW MANY KINDS OF MOSQUITOES ARE THERE?

Too many! There are more than 2,500 types of mosquito worldwide. They tend to live in hot, humid places.

ARE THERE BUGS THAT EAT SKIN?

Harvest mite larvae are tiny orange parasites that love to eat your skin. They inject digestive juices into you to make a well of liquefied skin cells that they can then suck up, then drop off when they're done.

WHO LAYS GLUEY EGGS?

Female head lice use a super-sticky protein to glue their eggs onto hair strands. You can shake your head, wash your hair, or swim underwater—those eggs won't budge!

WHAT MAKES FLEAS HATCH?

Flea eggs don't hatch unless there is a host nearby to feast on.

ARE ELEPHANTS TO BLAME FOR ELEPHANTIASIS?

No. The wuchereria parasitic worm causes elephantiasis, a disfiguring disease where the limbs swell alarmingly and the skin thickens and becomes ulcerated.

DO ALL FLEAS JUMP?

At just 1mm (0.04in) long, the tropical chigoe flea is the smallest known flea. Unlike other fleas, it is terrible at jumping.

HOW IS MALARIA SPREAD?

Some types of mosquito have a parasite in their saliva that is passed on when they bite, which causes a disease called malaria. Malaria kills more than one million people every year.

WHAT IS THE WORST KIND OF WORM TO GET?

The worst worm infection you can get has to be tropical Guinea worm disease. Between one and two years after drinking infected water, a spaghetti-like worm up to 100cm (40in) long will pop out of a blister in the foot or leg. The only way to get a Guinea worm out of the skin safely is by wrapping it around a stick very ... very ... slowly, which can take up to a month!

HOW LONG DO LICE LIVE FOR?

Each female head louse lives for about a month, and can lay up to 150 eggs in that time.

DID YOU KNOW?

New York City had a bedbug epidemic in 2007, when a record 6,889 calls were made to pest control companies. The tiny brown pests infested top hotels, hospitals, cinemas, and schools, as well as homes.

WHERE DO DUST MITES LIVE?

You have at least a million dust mites crawling around your mattress and pillow, gobbling up all your old skin cells.

HOW ARE MAGGOTS GOOD FOR YOU?

Some maggots love to munch away at dead flesh! They leave healthy flesh alone, though, and this can be put to good use with "maggot therapy," where maggots are applied to wounds to help keep them clean as they heal.

WHAT IS SNAKE FLOSSING?

A man known as Snake Manu loves a bit of "snake flossing"—he puts slim snakes, including deadly cobras, up his nose and passes them out through his mouth.

CAN WORMS GET IN YOUR EYEBALLS?

Horseflies in West Africa spread the loa loa worm through their bites. The infection is also known as African eye worm, as the sufferer may feel the worms wriggling across their eyeballs. Eek!

WHY SHOULD YOU NOT STROKE CATERPILLARS?

Fluffy puss caterpillars look good enough to stroke, but poisonous spines are lurking under their soft hair. When touched, the spines lodge painfully in the skin, causing numbness, blisters, and a rash.

DID YOU KNOW?

Biologist Mike Leahy is so committed to his work that he volunteered to swallow a tapeworm for research purposes. By the time he got rid of it, the worm was 3m (10ft) long!

DID YOU KNOW?

Someone with a bad roundworm infection will vomit worms. Disgusting!

WHICH BEETLE GETS STUCK IN YOUR HAIR?

The largest beetle in New Zealand is the Huhu and it can give you a nasty nip with its strong jaws! Its other name is the "haircutter"—if one gets tangled in your hair, it has to be cut out with scissors!

WHAT IS A ZOONOSIS?

A zoonosis is an infectious disease that can be transferred between animals and people, such as bird flu.

WHAT IS THE MOST COMMON FLEA?

The most common flea worldwide is the cat flea ... which is just as happy sucking human blood, if it can't find a cat.

WHY ARE TICKS HARD TO REMOVE?

Ticks plunge barbs into the skin of their host to keep them anchored in place. That's why they're so difficult to remove!

DID YOU KNOW?

Head lice are sensitive to heat and will abandon the head of someone with a fever.

WHAT HAPPENS IF LICE DRINK TOO MUCH?

Greedy young head lice can die from overfeeding, as their tiny guts spring a leak if they drink too much of your blood.

WHY SHOULD YOU WATCH WHERE YOU GO SWIMMING?

Bilharzia is a flatworm infection that can be caught by paddling or swimming in tropical lakes. It can damage the stomach, bladder, and liver, so think carefully next time you're tempted to go for a swim on vacation!

DID YOU KNOW?

Leeches carry viruses, bacteria, and parasites from their previous hosts, and pass them on to subsequent victims.

WHAT DOES A TICK BITE FEEL LIKE?

Nobody knows! A tick's saliva contains a natural painkiller, which is why you can't feel it biting.

DID YOU KNOW?

More than a billion people have a hookworm infection, which means they have tiny blood-sucking worms living in their intestines. Altogether, those hookworms suck a total of 10 million L (22 million pt) of blood a day!

ARE SWEAT BEES SWEATY?

No. Sweat bees are so called because they love the salt in your sweat! Don't worry—their sting is almost painless compared to that of other bees.

WHICH INFECTION GIVES YOU BAD BURPS?

One nasty symptom of giardiasis is foul burps that can be so bad they induce vomiting! The infection is caused by a parasite with tentacle-like limbs.

DID YOU KNOW?

1.5 billion people around the world have ascariasis, an infection in which earthworm-like parasites can grow as long as 30cm (12in) inside the intestine.

DID YOU KNOW?

Forensic entomologists can work out when someone died by examining the maggots and beetles on their corpse.

WHICH BUGS LIKE DANDRUFF?

Dust mites love a bit of dandruff, and like to take up residence in a flaky scalp!

WHY SHOULD YOU AVOID EMPTY BIRD NESTS?

If you find an empty bird nest, leave it alone. It could contain bird mites—and in spite of their name, these creatures are not fussy about drinking human blood!

DID YOU KNOW?

There are 2,000 types of flea on the planet.

WHY DO HEAD LICE LIKE CLEAN HAIR?

Head lice prefer clean hair to dirty hair, as it's easier for them to grip onto.

ARE LEECHES EASY TO REMOVE?

Some leeches just won't let go! One Hong Kong woman had to have one surgically removed from her nostril, when it clung on for weeks after she washed her face in an infested stream. The nose invader was 5cm (2in) long.

DID YOU KNOW?

Cellulitis is a skin reaction that can follow an insect bite. The area around the bite swells alarmingly and has to be treated with antibiotics.

WHAT DOES A FIRE ANT BITE FEEL LIKE?

The bite of a fire ant feels like a nasty burn on your skin, and turns into an itchy white blister.

DID YOU HEAR ABOUT THE GUY WHO TOOK HIS SNAKE TO A BANK?

In 2004, a South African man purposely released deadly puff adders into the bank that repossessed his car. A cleaner was bitten and the man was charged with attempted murder.

HOW TINY ARE THREADWORM EGGS?

Threadworm eggs are so small that you can't see them. They can float through the air, so you can catch worms if the eggs zoom up your nose when you breathe in!

WHAT SPREAD THE BLACK DEATH?

Rat fleas spread the bubonic plague—the so-called "Black Death." Although it's rare these days, the illness killed around one third of the population of 14th-century Europe.

HOW LONG WAS THE LONGEST TAPEWORM?

The biggest tapeworm ever found in a person's intestine was 25m (82ft) long. That's as long as two buses end to end!

HOW LONG IS LUNCH FOR A LEECH?

It takes 20 minutes for a leech to fill itself up with blood. Leeches secrete an enzyme that stops blood from clotting as they feed. They usually drop off once they're full, but the bite carries on bleeding until the clot-stopping substance has been washed away.

WHY WOULD YOU HAVE TO BE BRAVE TO FACE A BULLET ANT?

The most painful ant bite comes from the bullet ant. Some Amazonian tribesmen purposely put these ants on their skin during rituals to test their bravery.

DID YOU KNOW?

Intestinal myiasis basically means maggots in the stomach! The maggots can be swallowed in infected food and cause stomach pains, but are eventually digested by gastric juices. That doesn't sound fun, does it?

DID YOU KNOW?

40 million Americans have threadworms at any one time.

STRANGE BUT TRUE

ARE HAIR CLIPPINGS USEFUL?

American barber Bill Black saved the hair clippings swept up from his floor, and used them to make vests, shirts, ties, and even a bikini! Sounds itchy!

WHAT ELSE CAN HUMAN HAIR BE USED FOR?

Human hair clippings have also been used to help contain oil spills. In 2007, mats woven from hair were used to soak up oil at San Francisco's Ocean Beach.

DID YOU KNOW?

Australian rugby player Jamie Ainscough suffered a severe arm infection that puzzled doctors. The mystery was solved when an X-ray revealed an opponent's tooth stuck under his skin!

Australian performance artist Stelarc had a human ear grafted onto his forearm in the name of art. He can literally turn a deaf ear to anyone who annoys him!

WHO HAS THE BAGGIEST EARLOBES?

Hawaiian Kala Kaiwi used wooden discs to stretch the holes in his earlobes to an eye-watering 10cm (4in) across.

DID YOU KNOW?

When Dharmendra Singh of Rajasthan, India, smokes a cigarette, the smoke comes out of his ears.

WHO PLAYED TUNES WITH HIS BOTTOM?

British entertainer Mr. Methane described himself as "the world's only full-time performing flatulist." Yep, people paid to hear him fart tunes!

WHICH FISHERMAN BECAME BAIT?

Peter Hodge—also from Britain—was a keen angler and wanted to be fed to the fish when he died. His ashes were mixed with fish food and thrown into the River Huntspill.

DID YOU KNOW?

Reclusive billionaire Howard Hughes had such a phobia of germs that his staff had to cover his cutlery handles with layers of tissue paper and cellophane.

WHY SHOULD YOU ALWAYS CHECK A DENTIST'S QUALIFICATIONS?

When Italian police investigated complaints against dentist-from-hell Alvaro Perez, they discovered he had been using a regular power drill on his patients, and had no dental qualifications at all.

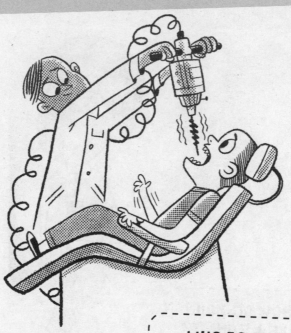

DID YOU KNOW?

Some African cultures engage in scarification, when patterns of raised scars are made on the skin as decoration, or to show bravery.

WHO IS THE LIZARDMAN?

American performance artist "The Lizardman" has a forked tongue, green-inked lips, sharpened teeth, and green scales tattooed on his body.

HOW DID A NAIL GUN CAUSE A TOOTHACHE?

When American carpenter Patrick Lawler visited the dentist complaining of a toothache, an X-ray revealed a 10-cm (4-in) nail lodged in his brain. His nail gun had backfired while he was working, but he had not realized that he had been injured. What a tough guy!

HOW DO YOU FAKE A ZOMBIE?

Zombies really do exist—in a manner of speaking! Haitian witch doctors called bokors can use plant-based drugs to make a person appear to be dead, then revive them.

WHO IS KING OF THE BIG MAC?

American burger enthusiast Don Gorske scoffed 23,000 Big Macs in 36 years. He even has the receipts to prove it!

WHEN SHOULD YOU AVOID TAKING THE TRAIN?

The annual Mooning Amtrak event involves thousands of people showing their bottoms to passing trains in California. The organizers especially welcome decorated and plus-size butts!

WHICH DOCTOR HAD BACTERIA FOR LUNCH?

Australian doctor Barry Marshall insisted that stomach ulcers were not caused by stress or spicy foods, but by the bacterium helicobacter pylori. He proved his point by swallowing a Petri dish full of it!

WHO LEFT MORE THAN FINGERPRINTS AT A CRIME SCENE?

A Swiss thief whose finger was cut off by broken glass was caught when police found the finger at the crime scene, and matched its print with their records.

WHAT HAPPENS TO YOUR BODY ON A ROLLERCOASTER?

If you feel like your stomach has dropped when you're on a rollercoaster, it's because it has! Your body reacts to the G-force on a rollercoaster, meaning that your insides actually move around.

WHY SHOULDN'T YOU BITE YOUR NAILS?

British man Richard Ross was holding a nail (not a fingernail, a metal one!) between his lips while doing DIY, when he inhaled it! His ribs had to be broken to remove it.

DID YOU KNOW?

After spending five days with his arm trapped under a fallen boulder, mountaineer Aron Ralston had to take drastic action—he cut off his arm with a penknife. His bravery has been immortalized in the movie *127 Hours*.

WHO WAS ARRESTED FOR FARTING?

Following his arrest for drink-driving, American José Cruz was charged with assault when he farted on a police officer. In his statement, the officer complained that "the gas was very odorous."

DID YOU KNOW?

Several people have been injured or drowned trying to go over the edge of Niagara Falls. (And it's illegal, anyway).

WHEN WAS A HEDGEHOG A WEAPON?

New Zealander William Singalargh was arrested for using a hedgehog as an offensive weapon—he threw it at a youth, causing scratches and puncture wounds.

WHO LIKES TO PAINT THEIR TEETH?

The Si La people of Laos have an old tradition of painting their teeth. Men have red teeth and women have black.

DID YOU KNOW?

After Czech President Vaclav Claus had a hip replacement operation, a police investigation began. His original hip had been put up for sale on an auction website!

WHO WEARS THE HEAVIEST EARRINGS?

Some cultures have a tradition of earlobe stretching—people wear heavy earrings that can weigh up to half a kg (1lb) and hang them from huge holes in their earlobes.

WHAT ARE FINGERNAILS FOR?

Fingernails play an important role in protecting some of the most sensitive parts of your body. They also stop the flesh of your fingertips from being pushed back when you grasp objects. Handy!

DID YOU KNOW?

Estonians have an age-old saying—if you point at a rainbow, your finger will fall off.

DID YOU KNOW?

Chinese man Li Jianping has been growing his fingernails for more than 15 years ... but only on his left hand! Their total length is more than 1m (3ft), and he avoids crowded places in case he breaks one.

CAN YOU GROW TEETH IN A LAB?

Yes, scientists have found a way to grow teeth! So far, only parts of a tooth have been grown from stem cells, but farmed teeth could replace false ones in the future.

DID YOU KNOW?

The record for the longest moustache in the world belongs to Ram Singh Chauhan, whose facial hair measures a jaw-dropping 4.29m (14ft).

WHERE DO ADULT TEETH COME FROM?

Adult teeth start to develop in babies' jaws while they still have their milk teeth. Both sets of teeth can be seen on X-rays!

WHERE CAN YOU DONATE YOUR HAIR?

Pilgrims to the Tirupati temple in India give their hair as a sacrifice. The temple's 600 barbers shave thousands of visitors every day, taking 6.5 million hairy gifts every year.

DID YOU KNOW?

Women of the Ethiopian Surma tribe have an old tradition of putting a clay disk in their bottom lip to stretch it outward. The lower teeth have to be removed first.

WHY IS SLEEP IMPORTANT?

Everyone knows that a good night's sleep can help you to concentrate. But sleep has many other benefits, too. Did you know that a lack of sleep can make you more likely to put on weight, and less able to fight disease?

People travel from all over the world to enter the annual tongue-tingling Nettle Eating Championships in Dorset, England.

DID YOU KNOW?

American politician Stan Jones drank a homemade silver solution in the belief that it would boost his immune system. It made his skin take on a silver hue!

CAN YOU WRITE WITH YOUR EYES?

Chinese man Ru Anting can write on paper with water squirted from his eyes! He decided to hone his eye-spraying skill for entertainment when he lost his factory job.

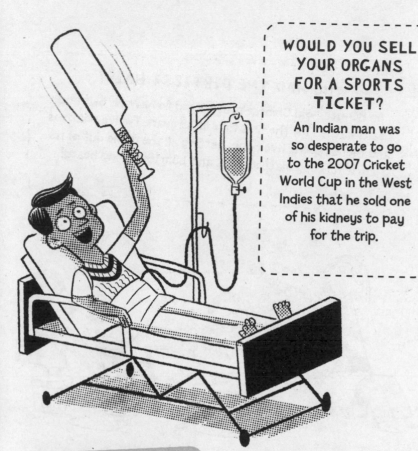

WOULD YOU SELL YOUR ORGANS FOR A SPORTS TICKET?

An Indian man was so desperate to go to the 2007 Cricket World Cup in the West Indies that he sold one of his kidneys to pay for the trip.

IS SPITTING DUNG A SPORT?

One way to pass the time in some parts of Africa is to take part in some kudu dung spitting. The sport involves spitting pellets of antelope dung as far as you can!

WHAT'S ON THE MENU?

Artist Marco Evaristti held a dinner party and served meatballs made with his own liposuction fat!

WHO HAD THE DIRTIEST HAIR?

An 80-year-old Chinese man agreed to have his hair and beard washed for the first time in 23 years. Twelve relatives and friends spent five hours getting all the grime out of his 2m (6ft)-long matted locks and 1.5m (5ft)-long beard!

DID YOU KNOW?

Argentinian artist Nicola Constantino used fat removed from her own body to make 100 bars of soap and two sculptures.

DID YOU KNOW?

Chinese man Zhang Yinming can snort milk up his nose and squirt it out of his eyes to a distance of up to 2m (6ft).

WHO HAS THE BIGGEST NOSTRILS?

Himalayan Apatani tribeswomen used to enlarge their nostrils with 2.5cm (1in)-wide circular nose plugs.

WHICH MOUNTAINEER BRRRRR-AVED THE ELEMENTS?

On reaching the top of Mount Everest, Lakpa Tharke Sherpa took all his clothes off for three whole minutes. Chilly!

WHO HAS THE BIGGEST COLLECTION OF BELLY-BUTTON FLUFF?

Australian Graham Barker has 24 years' worth of his belly-button fluff saved in storage jars. What a strange collection!

WHOSE BOTTOM LED TO AN ARREST?

German bank robber Sandra Meiser tried to hold up the same bank branch twice. She was caught the second time, when a witness recognized her large bottom!

DID YOU KNOW?

The highlight of the year in the Japanese city of Shibukawa is the Belly Button Festival. People dance in the streets with faces painted on their stomachs.

DID YOU KNOW?

In the USA, more than 150 pairs of identical twins are married to identical twins.

WHO MADE ART FROM HIS TOENAILS?

For his "Only You" exhibition, Uruguayan artist Carlos Capelán created collages made from his toenail clippings.

WHO TOOK 40 YEARS TO GET A HAIRCUT?

At the age of 15, British girl Jean Burgess decided that she would never have her hair cut again. When she reached 55, her hair was 1.65m (5ft 6in) long and took more than two hours to comb!

DID YOU KNOW?

American sideshow performer Enigma has had surgery to give him horns on his head. He has a jigsaw puzzle tattoo that covers his whole body, too.

WHOSE POOP WAS AS PRICEY AS GOLD?

Italian artist Piero Manzoni filled 90 small tins with his own poop for a 1961 exhibition. They were sold to art buyers at a price equal to their weight in gold!

ARE THERE RAT POLICE?

Police in Soweto, South Africa, had to deal with a series of assaults ... by giant rats! The oversized rodents were nesting in old cars and attacking passers-by.

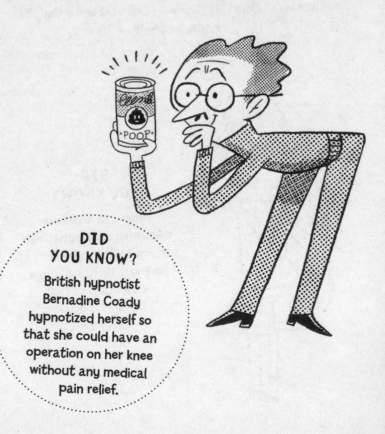

DID YOU KNOW?

British hypnotist Bernadine Coady hypnotized herself so that she could have an operation on her knee without any medical pain relief.

WHERE ARE LONG NECKS MOST ATTRACTIVE?

Thai Karen tribeswomen traditionally wear several neck rings to lengthen their necks. The first bands are added at the age of five, and more are added every few months.

DID YOU KNOW?

A British man called Garry Turner holds the odd title of having the world's stretchiest skin! He has a rare condition called Ehlers-Danlos Syndrome, which means he can stretch his skin to a length of 15.8cm (6.25in).

WHAT CAN YOU DO IF YOU DON'T LIKE YOUR BIRTHMARKS?

American Matt Gone hated his birthmarks so much that he had his body covered in a checkerboard pattern to hide them. That's 500 hours' worth of tattoos!

WHICH ARTIST FELT DRAINED BY HIS WORK?

English artist Marc Quinn made a model of his head from 4L (8pt) of his own deep-frozen blood. The blood for the work, entitled "Self," was collected over five months.

DID YOU KNOW?

In 2002, Polish anatomist Gunther von Hagens carried out the first public autopsy in 170 years. Over 500 people paid to watch him cut open a body, before removing its internal organs.

HOW CAN YOU BECOME AN ARTWORK AFTER DEATH?

Several people have donated their bodies to Gunther von Hagens so that he can plastinate (preserve and dissect) them for his Body Worlds exhibitions.

MALADIES AND MALFUNCTIONS

WHAT MAKES YOUR PEE GO BLACK?

Blackwater fever is so called because its sufferers pass black urine. The rare phenomenon, known as Blaschko's lines, is characterized by pigmented stripes on a person's skin, particularly across the back.

WHAT DO YOU DO BEFORE VOMITING?

Ever wondered why you salivate before throwing up? It's your body's way of protecting your teeth from the high acid levels in vomit.

WHAT CAUSES A BRUISE?

A bruise is a blood leak under your skin—a bigger leak makes a bigger bruise.

WHAT HAPPENS IF YOU GET TOO MUCH EARWAX?

A head injury or earwax build-up can cause tinnitus—a ringing, whistling, or hissing noise in one or both ears ... all the time!

WHAT IS BLACK HAIRY TONGUE?

It's a fungal infection that causes the taste buds to swell and darken, giving the tongue a black, furry appearance.

DID YOU KNOW?

People with the rare condition Naegeli Syndrome have no fingerprints.

WHAT IS MONKEY POX?

Monkey pox is similar to chickenpox. The difference is that you catch monkeypox from monkeys, but you catch chickenpox from ... humans!

DO CAULIFLOWERS HAVE EARS?

The strange lumps on some rugby players' ears are known as "cauliflower ear." They are caused by blood clots forming on the ear after being hit, or by skin being torn from the ear's cartilage.

HOW DO YOU GET SAUSAGE FINGERS?

If a person's liver isn't working properly, their hands can swell up so that their fingers look like fat sausages. The condition is known as clubbing.

DID YOU KNOW?

Glue ear is when the ear fills with goo, which dulls the hearing, but is surprisingly painless!

HOW DO YOU GET BLUE SKIN?

People with the enzyme deficiency methemoglobinemia have blue skin, as their blood carries much less oxygen than it should. Oxygenated blood is bright red.

CAN YOU GET BAD BREATH IN YOUR NOSE?

Bad breath doesn't just come from the mouth—a sinus infection can make whiffy air come out of the nose, too!

WHOSE HICCUPS LASTED OVER A YEAR?

Singer Christopher Sands had a bout of hiccups that lasted for 15 months! He was finally cured by an operation to replace a faulty valve in his stomach.

WHAT IS RAT-BITE FEVER?

Rat-bite fever is caught from rodent bites or rodent urine, and causes a high temperature, headache, vomiting, and agonizing joint pains.

HOW CAN BABY PEE HELP BOXERS?

Swollen hands are an occupational hazard for boxers, but Ukrainian boxer Vitali Klitschko has his own remedy—baby pee! He says that his son's wet nappies reduce the swelling when he wraps them around his fists after a match.

CAN PEE HELP WITH JELLYFISH STINGS?

Some people think that pouring pee on a jellyfish sting can make it less painful—while others recommend vinegar. However, there is no scientific evidence for either of these ideas.

ARE THERE REALLY WEREWOLVES?

Someone with hypertrichosis, or Werewolf Syndrome, has extra-long hair all over their body, including their face.

WHAT IS SCURVY?

Many sailors of the past suffered from a vitamin C deficiency, known as scurvy, which gave them spongy gums, loose teeth, and purple blotches on their skin.

DID YOU KNOW?

People with microcephaly have heads that are much smaller than average.

WHAT ARE SWOLLEN GLANDS?

The swollen "glands" that you get when you're ill are actually your lymph nodes—they can swell to the size of an orange when they're fighting an infection.

CAN BULLFROGS FIGHT SUPERBUGS?

Scientific tests have shown that a protein secreted by bullfrogs could wipe out MRSA, one of the nasty "superbugs" that lurk in some hospitals.

WHO WAS THE WORLD'S MEANEST MOTHER?

Penny-pinching multimillionaire Hetty Green would not pay for her son to have his broken leg treated. He then got gangrene and had to have the limb amputated.

DID YOU KNOW?

An American study showed that there is an 18 percent increase in fatal road accidents on presidential election days.

WHY SHOULD YOU AVOID REPTILE POOP?

Pet reptiles may seem like fun, but they can be hazardous—nine out of ten reptiles have salmonella bacteria in their poop, which can be passed on to owners and cause serious illness.

WHAT IS LOCKJAW?

Tetanus causes facial spasms and stops the mouth opening, which is why the disease is also known as "lockjaw."

CAN YOU SURVIVE BEING STRUCK BY LIGHTNING?

Yes, you certainly can. Each year, about 500 people around the world are struck by lightning, and of those 500, 450 survive. That said, lightning can cause serious injuries. One of the stranger effects is called "lightning flowers." That's when a strike breaks blood vessels in the skin, creating red, snaky patterns.

WHAT IS LASER EYE SURGERY?

During laser eye surgery, a cut is made in the eye and a laser is used to change the shape of the cornea ... while the patient is awake!

WHAT VIRUS GIVES YOU HAMSTER CHEEKS?

The mumps virus causes painful swelling of the salivary glands and gives sufferers puffed-out "hamster cheeks."

DID YOU KNOW?

Acne is not contagious and is not affected by whether the skin is clean or not—in fact, too much washing can make it worse.

CAN A BUMP ON THE HEAD CHANGE YOUR NATIONALITY?

Of course not! However, it could make you sound like you're from another part of the world. This strange injury is called "foreign accent syndrome."

WHAT IS SPACE SICKNESS?

Space sickness is the mother of all motion sickness—the lack of gravity confuses the brain, causing headaches, nausea, loss of balance, and feelings of confusion.

WHY ARE FEVERS GOOD FOR YOU?

Most bacteria and viruses that invade your body have evolved to be most effective at 37°C/98.6°F. A fever is your body's way of killing them off!

WHAT CAN MAKE YOUR EYES GO BLACK?

Someone with the rare condition aniridia has no irises, so their eyes look completely black, like big pupils.

CAN YOU BE ALLERGIC TO MOBILE PHONES?

Yes! A person with a nickel allergy will develop a rash when their skin comes into contact with any buttons or handsets that are made from the metal.

WHAT IS A GOITER?

A lack of the mineral iodine in your diet makes your thyroid gland swell up, creating a large lump in your neck, known as a goiter.

WHAT IS HYPERMOBILITY?

About one quarter of people have joints that are more flexible than usual. This is called hypermobility or double-jointedness. In most cases, it is completely harmless—and can even be impressive! Professional contortionists turn their hypermobility into a performance art.

DID YOU KNOW?

A high fever can cause an unpleasant sensation called formication—it feels as if ants are crawling all over your skin!

HAS VACCINATION ENDED ANY DISEASES?

Smallpox is the only human infectious disease to have been completely wiped out through vaccination.

IS WEB BROWSING GOOD FOR YOU?

Surfing the internet boosts brainpower! A University of California study showed that using the web stimulates the decision-making and reasoning parts of the brain.

DID YOU KNOW?

Verrucas that grow in clusters are known as mosaic warts.

HOW CAN YOU LOSE YOUR SENSES?

People with anosmia have no sense of smell and very little sense of taste. This not only makes life a little dull, it can be dangerous—they can't smell signs of danger, such as smoke or gas.

WHY ARE COFFINS GETTING BIGGER?

More obese people in the world means bigger coffins—one British council had to install extra-large furnaces in its crematoriums to accommodate 1m (3ft)-wide coffins.

WHAT IS CRADLE CAP?

Cradle cap is the crusty, yellow, scaly stuff on a young baby's scalp. You might think it looks yucky, but it doesn't bother the baby!

WHAT DOES YOUR SNOT TELL YOU?

Nose mucus is normally clear and runny, but if you have a bacterial infection it can turn thick and yellow, or even green!

CAN YOU GET BLUE PUS?

Some infections can produce blue pus. The freaky shade comes from a bacteria called pseudomonas.

WHY DO POLAR EXPLORERS GET FROSTBITE?

When explorers are not able to keep their hands and feet warm, so little blood reaches their extremities in subzero temperatures that their fingers and toes can rot and turn black. They will need to be amputated if this happens.

DID YOU KNOW?

Indonesian fisherman Dede Koswara suffers from a rare genetic disorder—his body reacted to a wart virus by covering his skin with huge growths that look like tree bark.

DID YOU KNOW?

Lakshmi Tatma was born with an extra pair of arms and legs. Thirty doctors worked for 24 hours to successfully remove her spare limbs.

DID YOU KNOW?

Severe vomiting can burst the blood vessels around the eyes and cause a black eye.

WHAT HAPPENS WHEN YOU SNEEZE?

More than 40,000 droplets are sprayed into the air when you sneeze. If you have any infectious germs, it's a very effective way of spreading them!

CAN YOU SURVIVE "EXPLODING HEAD SYNDROME?"

Exploding head syndrome isn't quite as gruesome as it sounds—it's a severe form of tinnitus. Sufferers hear a loud but imaginary explosion while falling asleep.

WHY ARE BLISTERS SQUASHY?

Blisters are squidgy because they're full of lymph and other body fluids.

DID YOU KNOW?

Russian Alexander Sizonenko can't stop growing! The former basketball player suffers from gigantism and was 2.44m (8ft) tall when last measured.

WHY DO SKIERS WEAR SUNGLASSES?

You may think that sunglasses are more suited to the beach than snowy mountains, but skiers have to take care to protect their eyes. Snow blindness occurs when the eyes are sunburnt by the strong sunlight reflected off snow or ice.

WHAT IS STRAWBERRY TONGUE?

One symptom of scarlet fever is strawberry tongue—the tongue swells up and turns bright red, making it look like a strawberry.

WHERE CAN YOU FIND A SPARE CORNEA?

A damaged cornea can be replaced in a straightforward cornea transplant operation, but the new cornea has to come from a fresh corpse.

WHO WANTS UNNECESSARY OPERATIONS?

British man William McIloy had 400 operations ... that he didn't need! He had a disorder called Munchausen syndrome, which makes people fake severe illness to get medical attention.

DID YOU KNOW?

Nasal polyps are fleshy growths in the nostril that can affect the sense of smell—a big one can be the size of a grape!

COULD TOO MUCH CHOCOLATE BE FATAL?

Yes—but only in theory! The toxic chemicals in 10kg (2lb) of chocolate would kill you ... but trying to eat that much food would make you vomit.

WHOSE GOAL CELEBRATION WAS THE MOST PAINFUL?

When soccer player Paulo Diogo tried to jump over a barrier during a goal celebration, his wedding ring got caught and he lost the top half of his finger. The referee even gave him a yellow card for wasting time!

DID YOU KNOW?

The black dot in the middle of a verruca is its blood supply.

WHY DOES A COLD MAKE YOUR NOSE RUN?

Snot—or mucus, to use its proper name—protects your body by capturing airborne viruses and bacteria. When you are infected by a cold virus, more mucus is made for extra protection.

WHO SPENT 30 YEARS SMELLING OF FISH?

After 30 years of smelling like stale fish, a 41 year-old Australian woman finally had her rare disorder diagnosed. Rimethylaminuria affects the smell of sweat, breath, and urine—and has the strange effect of making people smell fishy.

WHAT CAN GIVE YOU REALLY STINKY BREATH?

A bad gum infection called gingivitis can lead to pus-filled mouth sores, purple gums, and the stinkiest of stinky breath.

WHAT ARE CARBUNCLES?

Are you sure you want to know? Carbuncles are swollen, pus-filled lumps of skin that can be as big as golf balls—and what's even worse, they're contagious!

HOW DO YOU GET HEAT RASH?

Plugged-up sweat glands cause prickly heat rash in hot weather—fresh sweat gets trapped and forms a prickling, itchy rash of tiny blisters.

WHICH OF YOUR JOINTS IS THE MOST MOBILE?

Your shoulder joint is the most mobile joint in your body. The bad news is that it's also the easiest joint to dislocate!

DID YOU KNOW?

Moldova has the highest rate of fatal lawnmower accidents.

WHAT HAPPENS WHEN SCARS HEAL TOO MUCH?

The formation of scar tissue following a skin injury can go haywire and create a rubbery growth called a keloid.

DID YOU KNOW?

An early typhus vaccine was made from squished body lice infected with the deadly disease!

WHAT IS THE WORLD'S LARGEST PARASITE?

The largest parasite that infects humans is the fish tapeworm. It can live for up to 20 years, and one adult worm sheds up to a million eggs a day— the biggest one ever recorded was 18m (60ft) long!

WHAT WAS AN EARLY CURE FOR WARTS?

Medieval wart sufferers used to rub their ugly growths with a piece of raw meat and then bury it. They believed that as the meat rotted away, the warts would also disappear. Warts eventually go away by themselves anyway, so that's why everyone thought it worked!

DID YOU KNOW?

Whiskey distillery founder Jack Daniel kicked his safe in a temper when he couldn't open it, and died from the resulting toe infection. Some say that if he'd dipped the toe in his own whiskey, he would have been fine!

CAN HONEY HEAL WOUNDS?

Some ancient remedies did work. In the past, wounds were often treated with honey and willow bark—honey is a natural antiseptic and willow contains the painkiller that is in aspirin.

CAN SUNLIGHT MAKE YOU SNEEZE?

Some people react to bright sunlight by sneezing. This is called photic sneezing and is inherited, so you can blame your parents if it happens to you!

WHEN CAN ACUPUNCTURE GO TOO FAR?

Chinese doctor Wei Shengchu set a record in 2004 when he had 1,790 acupuncture needles stuck into his head and face.

DID YOU KNOW?

The name of the lung disease pneumonoultramicroscopic -silicovolcanoconiosis is the longest word in the English language.

HOW BIG IS YOUR APPENDIX?

The length of an average appendix is around 10cm (4in), but the largest ever was removed from a Croatian man and measured 26cm (10.2in) long!

WHO HAS THE MOST TATTOOS?

New Zealander Lucky Diamond Rich is tattooed on every inch of his body, including his gums and inside his ears. He even has tattoos on his tattoos!

DID YOU KNOW?

Bobby Leach was the first man to go over Niagara Falls in a barrel, surviving his multiple injuries. He went out with less of a fanfare, dying from gangrene after slipping on some orange peel.